Bully Proof
Bedtime Healing Meditation for Children

Little Blue Zen

BULLY PROOF

Copyright@ 2024 Jo Galloway

The right of the author has been asserted to her following the copyright writing, designs and patent act of Australia.

All rights reserved. No part of this book may be reproduced, stored or transmitted by any means whether auditory, graphic, mechanical, or electronic without the written permission of the author. Unauthorised reproduction of any part of this work is illegal and is punishable by law.

Unless otherwise noted, the author and the publisher make no explicit guarantees as the accuracy of the information contained in this book may differ based on individual experiences and context

ISBN: 978-1-7635801-0-7

Published by Little Blue Zen
Birdwood NSW
Printed in Australia
Cover Design: Gagan Karunachandra
Editing: Kristine Gibson
jo@littlebluezen.com
http://www.littlebluezen.com

Bully Proof

Bedtime Healing Meditation for Children

Jo Galloway

Your child may like other books in this series

- The Magical Worry Balloon. Ending anxiety & worry.

- A Coat of Flying Colours. Passing your Exams.

- The Magical Treasure Hunt. Building Confidence

- I am Different, I am Me.

- Angelic Dreams. Meet your Guardian Angel

- Scared of the Dark.

- I Love School.

- Bedwetting. Dry Nights.

INTRODUCTION

Why Healing Meditations.

As children we make sense of our experiences based on our limited understanding and perception. We may misinterpret events or draw conclusions that form the basis of limiting beliefs that influence our entire life. These beliefs become ingrained over time, shaping our thoughts, feelings and behaviours well into adulthood unless consciously challenged.

In my work as a practicing Hypnotherapist, I've found that all my clients' concerns, whether rooted in fears, feelings of inadequacy, addictive behaviors, or other challenges, trace back to their early childhood experiences, interactions, and upbringing. It's important to note that these issues don't exclusively stem from abusive or dysfunctional environments; limiting beliefs can arise from various circumstances.

Parents or caregivers wield substantial influence in shaping our perceptions of ourselves and the world around us. Remarks, criticisms, or comparisons made by family members can foster beliefs about our capabilities, worthiness, or potential. Furthermore, interactions with peers, teachers, and authority figures also contribute to the formation of these beliefs. Repeated experiences of rejection or failure can solidify beliefs such as "I'm not good enough" or "I'm unworthy of love."

This realization ignited my passion for intervening at the source: working with children to prevent these beliefs from taking root and manifesting into significant challenges in adulthood. By addressing issues early on, we can guide children to develop into the best versions of themselves, free from the burden of limiting beliefs that could otherwise dominate their lives.

How Healing Meditation will help your child.

Teaching children meditation offers a multitude of benefits that can positively influence their daily lives and overall development. A regular mindfulness meditation practice provides valuable tools for managing stress, navigating emotions, and promoting overall well-being. Healing meditations, in particular, bolster your child's self-belief, helping to remove any resistance they may face in adulthood. This leads to a happier, more successful and fulfilling life.

Unlike traditional meditation, which often centres on relaxation, healing meditations go a step further by focusing on recovery, balance, and reprogramming a child's self-belief. These meditations use techniques such as breathing exercises, visualization, and guided imagery to not only foster deep relaxation but also reshape their mindset.

This targeted approach helps build a stronger sense of self-confidence and resilience. By integrating positive affirmations and emotional healing, healing meditations offer a distinct advantage over traditional methods, laying a powerful foundation for a child's future success and well-being.

Meditation can also be an effective part of your child's bedtime routine, helping to calm the mind and prepare the body for restful sleep. Techniques like guided imagery and deep breathing, as outlined in this book, can signal to the brain that it's time to wind down.

Sharing these calming moments at bedtime not only strengthens the bond between parent and child, but also creates a supportive and nurturing environment. It also sets a positive example, emphasizing the importance of self-care and mindfulness.

With patience and consistency, you can help your child develop a lifelong practice that supports their mental, emotional, and physical health. Give your child the gift of relaxation and imagination with this easy-to-read story designed to inspire and uplift.

BULLY PROOF

Drift into a peaceful sleep with your very own magical adventure! Once your child has experienced "BULLY PROOF," no bully can shake their confidence.

This transformative Healing Meditation nurtures inner strength, empowering your child to repel negative, hurtful words effortlessly. BULLY PROOF takes your child on a magical journey that helps them overcome fears, build confidence and embrace their inner strength.

As they drift into peaceful sleep, they awaken, imbued with greater confidence, bravery, and self-assurance. The imagery of an invisible bubble of protective light shields them from criticism and negativity. "BULLY PROOF" not only builds confidence but also eases worries, fostering a sense of security and resilience.

It's more than just a bedtime story—it's a tool for building emotional strength and self-love.

Guide your child to a peaceful night's sleep and a brighter tomorrow with this heartwarming and empowering bedtime experience.

Delivered in a slow, monotone voice, this story captivates and soothes. BULLY PROOF, is also available on YouTube, providing a soothing auditory experience children can enjoy at home, in the car, or anywhere they need a moment of relaxation.

Since our minds learn through repetition, the more often your child hears the positive suggestions woven into this story, the more effective the results will be.

Listen on YouTube

Bully Proof

It's bedtime, my shining star.

Climb in and cozy up.

Before you get too comfortable, let's have a big stretch.

Stretch your arms, your legs, your fingers and your toes.

Have a little wiggle.

When you're ready to relax, uncross your legs, place your hands gently by your sides and softly close your eyes.

We're about to go on a magical adventure.

On this magical journey, you can see perfectly well with your eyes closed.

So, let's imagine you are being swept along by a gentle breeze.

This soft wind is helping you to float along.

A big bright moon above is shining moonlight beams to light your way.

Looking down, you can see yourself lying very still.

Your bed holds you like a cuddle!

You feel warm and safe.

Snug as a bug in a rug.

Notice a warm blue mist covering your feet and toes.

Feel a tingling sensation in your toes, while your feet become warm and cozy.

Watch now as the magical mist changes colour to a beautiful golden yellow.

This sparkly golden mist travels up your legs towards your knees.

All the way to the top of your legs.

As the gold mist moves gently and slowly, your legs feel oh so heavy.

The harder you try to lift your legs, the heavier and heavier they feel.

The magical golden mist continues to move up over your body, over your tummy, rising higher and higher.

As the magical sparkly golden mist passes your belly, it turns to the colour green.

The soft green grass mist moves up your chest and over your shoulders.

Gliding down your arms, spreading out into your fingers.

You can feel your fingers tingle.

You're feeling so calm and sleepy!

Your body has become all floppy and floaty.

Floppy like a rag doll.

You notice the mist now turning to a soft lilac colour.

This new colour covers your face, your cheeks and forehead.

Your entire face, eyes and head are now so relaxed and peaceful.

Any sounds around you are fading.

You are drifting deeper and deeper into your dreams.

This beautiful rainbow mist is a magical sleeping powder.

You feel yourself become so sleepy, wrapped up in the warmth of this magical rainbow coloured mist.

You notice clouds above you sparkling with flashing lights of soft colours.

They look they sunbeams but mostly white.

These white lights are streaming down from the much mellow clouds above to form a shape.

A big round shape, just like a balloon.

The balloon turns to all the colours of a rainbow.

The magical thing about this balloon is, it belongs to you.

It is filled with magical protection.

This is your very own protective balloon of light.

You feel so special knowing this balloon was made just for you.

Now you can reach up and pull the balloon full of magical protective light down over your head, down over your body and right under your feet.

Surrounding yourself completely within the magical balloon of protective light.

You are now floating inside your magical bubble of light.

Feeling so happy and safe.

You know, that while you are inside your special protective bubble of light, you are safe, you are loved, and you are protected.

This bubble is your very own superhero bullet proof armour.

The rainbow balloon of white light is always with you.

You can call your magical rainbow balloon down around you whenever you need protection, or whenever you feel hurt.

When other kids say nasty, hurtful words to you.

Or when you feel scared, just call on your magical rainbow balloon.

Call it down with the words, "I call in my magical rainbow balloon to protect me now."

No one can see your rainbow balloon except you.

It is your very own invisible shield.

Any nasty, mean words will just bounce right off your rainbow balloon.

Mean words and bullying children cannot penetrate your magical balloon of protection.

You are safe and protected within your rainbow balloon.

You stand tall and know your protective balloon of superhero light is all around you.

You are strong within your balloon; your inner strength shines brightly.

You know you are good enough and smart enough, no matter what a bully may say.

Their nasty words just bounce right off your invisible magical rainbow balloon.

Nothing harmful or untrue can reach you.

You have the magic now to just smile and float away.

Your bubble, your warrior superhero shield, protects you from harm.

Nothing nasty or wrong can get to you.

You are safe; you are protected.

You are brave, powerful, and free.

You are a superhero.

Sometimes you may meet other kids or even adults that are not kind.

They may say nasty things to you, call you names, or maybe laugh at you.

Their power is to make other children feel bad.

Well, no more, because you are safe now from their nasty words.

Children that say nasty mean things do not like themselves.

That is why they are so mean; they are very unhappy.

Have you ever noticed that happy children are never mean?

So next time anyone tries to burst your bubble by saying nasty cruel words to you, you have your protection ready.

You can look right through them and feel sorry for them, for they have no happiness.

Because you know, they are incredibly sad and very unhappy.

Because they are unhappy, doesn't have to stop you from being happy.

Every day, you tell yourself just how happy and special you are.

You really like yourself.

You are especially important to your family because you are an amazing child.

Place a big smile on your face and be happy just for being you.

You love to run and play and laugh with all your friends.

Your magical powers have made you strong, brave and confident, with superhero powers all your own.

Your special bubble of light was made just for you.

It fits into your pocket and goes everywhere with you, like superman's cape.

Ready to pull out and protect you while being invisible to everyone else.

When other children's hurtful words try to burst your bubble, they are powerless because you know inside your bubble you are strong and protected.

You have your very own feelings and thoughts, which are all that matter now.

You stand tall inside your bubble, free from the nasty words because you are safe and strong.

If a bully ever tries to give you something, like a mean name, you don't have to accept it; you don't have to let it into your rainbow balloon.

This way the bullies can keep their rude names for themselves.

If you don't, accept what they are saying, well, who's holding the mean names now?

They are, so let them keep them.

You don't want them.

You don't believe their nasty words, anyway.

You don't let them into your magical rainbow balloon.

Because you are happy, confident and like yourself.

You feel good on the inside, all fuzzy, warm and happy.

This shows on your face and in your body.

You shine a beautiful bright light from within and everyone around you can see your light shining so brightly and they smile at your happiness.

Your bright light keeps the bullies away.

Their hurtful ways just bounce right off you and your rainbow balloon.

So, look in the mirror every day, stare into your beautiful shiny eyes and say, "I love you, I like you, I will always protect you.

I will never let anyone harm you."

"You are amazing.
You are my best friend.
I will always be kind to you."
You are your very own cheerleader.
Imagine if a bully told lies about you to your all friends.
Or they pushed you and call you mean hurtful names.
Here is what to say to them.
"Thank you for sharing that with me."
And what you are saying is, that's how you see things, but I don't have to let your words affect me.
You have the power within you.

Own that super-power of protection.
No one can push you around.
So, stand in your power.
Surround yourself with loving friends and family.
You are bully proof, strong, brave, courageous and fearless.
But most of all, you are your best friend, happy, loved and protected.
Your magical superpower is all around you and within you.
Stand tall and be proud of who you are.
Let the bullies know their gruel games or hurtful words do not affect you.

No bully can break the spell of your invisible, protective rainbow balloon.

If you encounter any kind of struggle, you remain calm and fearless.

You are the boss of your thoughts and your emotions.

Inside your beautiful rainbow balloon of protective light, you move through life fearlessly.

You wear your invisible bubble-like Superman's cape.

No one can harm you now, you just won't allow it.

You are a superhero!

You won't let anything nasty into your protective rainbow balloon.

If you listen closely, past the hurtful words, you can hear those nasty words bouncing right off your bubble.

You know, nothing bullies say can hurt you or upset you.

See yourself walking to school or playing in the playground, ignoring all the unhappy mean bullies.

Nothing they can say or do will break through your invisible protective balloon.

You have stopped reacting when they tease you.

Notice the look on their faces.

They are shocked, surprised, struggling to keep their cool.

They realise you cannot be teased or hurt by their words or actions anymore.

You now shrug them off and walk away.

So tonight, as you drift off into a wonderful peaceful sleep, you can dream the most magical dreams, all the way to the morning light.

Knowing tomorrow, at any time, night or day, anywhere you go, whenever you feel threatened, all you have do is breathe.

Surround yourself in your bully proof bubble of protective light and smile.

You are safe; you are strong, and you are protected.

So, knowing this and believing this, it is time to drift slowly off to sleep.

Good night, my beautiful Starlight.

Remember, you are brave; you are Bully Proof.

Sweet dreams.......

Also by Jo Galloway

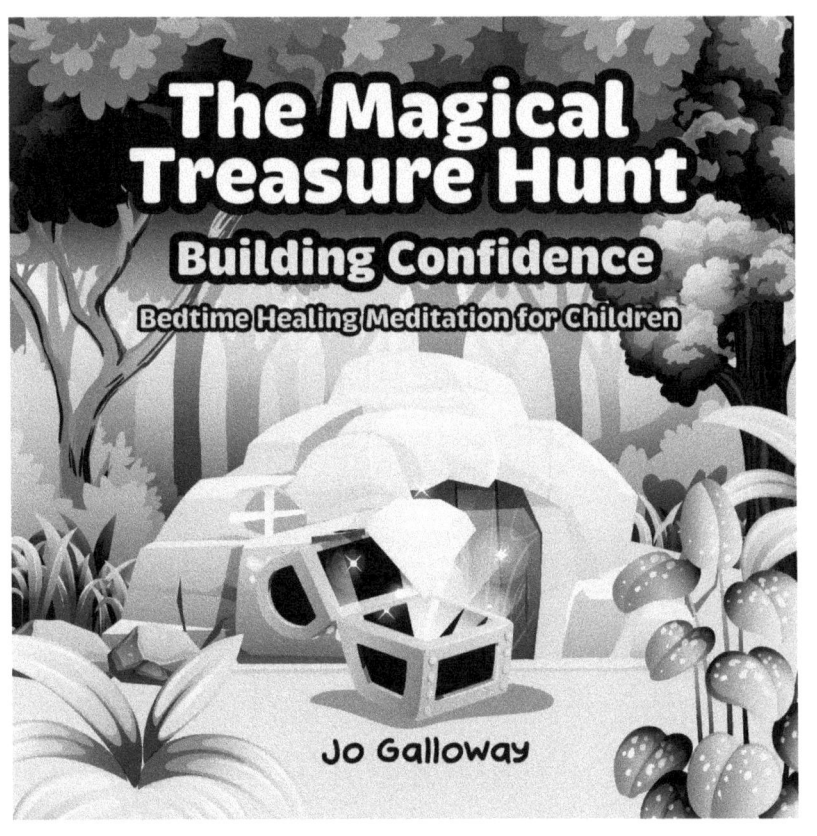

Embark on a whimsical journey with your little one as they venture into the world of self-discovery. As you guide your child through a series of relaxation exercises, they'll descend a rainbow staircase to meet their most cherished friend. Together they travel along an enchanted path. Here they'll uncover glittering stones inscribed with powerful messages: "I am lovable," "My body is beautiful just as it is," "I am good enough," and "I am confident."Each stone is a reminder of their unique strengths and worth, helping them embrace their true selves and shine with self-love and confidence.

Passing Your Exams

Sitting exams can often bring to the surface a child's self-sabotaging beliefs of I am not good enough, fears of failure or fear of rejection, along with bucket loads of anxiety.

Wearing the magical coat of Flying Colours is like wearing Superman's cape. This coat will transform your child's inner beliefs, allow access to their phenomenal memory, and enable them to remain calm and in total control while undertaking any exam.

Allow this gentle healing meditation to ease their worries, enhance their belief in their capabilities, empower their positivity to pass every exam with flying colours.

Little Blue Zen.com

Little Blue Zen

www.ingramcontent.com/pod-product-compliance
Lightning Source LLC
Chambersburg PA
CBHW042355070526
44585CB00028B/2942